DOUBLE YOUR SOLAR PUMP INSTALLATION, TRIPLE YOUR PROFIT

5 SECRETS TO SAVE TIME, MONEY AND EFFORT

DOUBLE YOUR SOLAR PUMP INSTALLATION, TRIPLE YOUR PROFIT

5 SECRETS TO SAVE TIME, MONEY AND EFFORT

Anirudh Agrawal

Available on amazonkindle

Worldwide Published by

Pendown Press
PREMIUM BUSINESS PUBLISHER

PENDOWN PRESS LLP
An ISO 9001 & ISO 14001 Certified Co.,
Regd. Office: 3767A, Kanhaiya Nagar,
Tri Nagar, Delhi-110035
Ph.: 8130886000, 9650072927
E-mail: info@pendownpress.com
Branch Office: 1A/2A, 20, Hari Sadan, Ansari Road,
Daryaganj, New Delhi-110002
Ph.: 011-45794768
Website: PendownPress.com

Edition: 2025
Price: ₹ 299
ISBN: 978-93-7217-276-8

Layout and Cover Designed by Pendown Graphics Team

For those who are looking to contribute
to India's growth journey in solar
pumping systems,

For those who are looking to accelerate solar
pump installation without hassle,

To the ones who keep building, learning, and
moving forward despite the odds,

This book is for you,

For your resilience, your commitment,
And the smarter, smoother growth
you truly deserve.

TABLE OF CONTENTS

PREFACE

Sometimes, all it takes is a quiet moment and an honest question: *"Is this really how it has to be?"*

This book began with a similar thought, not out of perfection, but out of curiosity... and maybe even a little frustration.

Over the years, I've met many system integrators: dedicated, skilled, and full of potential. A few of them were from leading companies contributing more than 50% to the PM Kusum Yojana.

Some system integrators, especially newcomers, I found were full of energy, potential, and passion, working day and night expecting massive outcomes.

But while meeting them and understanding the troubles stopping them from scaling faster, I found that they get stuck, sometimes unsure about their growth journey.

So, the intent of this book is to make a system integrator's life easier, without any hassle, while helping them double their revenue with ease and joy. And if you're holding this book, maybe you're one of them.

This book is my humble attempt to change that.

I'm not here to promise magic formulas. What I am offering is a fresh way of looking at things, a shift in perspective that can help you unlock what's already inside you. My only goal through these pages is to help system integrators scale their solar pumping business hassle-free and contribute to India's growth journey sustainably.

If this book can help you do even a little of that, it will have served its purpose.

Thank you for trusting me with your time. I hope what you find here feels like a conversation with an old friend, one who believes in you, sees your potential, and gently nudges you toward it.

Warm regards,

Anirudh

Acknowledgements

Whatever I have achieved in life would have been impossible without the support of my parents. They've taught me unconditional love, and I have seen them grow along with me. The wings I have today would not have been possible without them.

To my wife, Ankita, who has stood by me in every situation: you have handled all family responsibilities with great skill and dedication. Thank you from the bottom of my heart.

To my children, Krish and Mira, who are the source of my happiness and inspiration, lots of love!

My heartfelt gratitude to all my mentors and guides who have shown me light and direction in times of confusion.

To valued clients, who have shared their wide experiences and knowledge with me during this journey: thank you for trusting me and being our true inspiration and lighthouse in our growth journey.

A special acknowledgement goes to Dinesh Verma and his exceptional team at Pendown Press. From the initial concept to the final manuscript, their support and expertise have made this book possible.

And finally, to all my loved ones who have been with me on this journey: thank you for your unwavering support, encouragement, and affection. Even if your names are not mentioned, you always hold a special place in my heart.

Without the support of all of you, it would not have been possible for me to move forward with confidence.

AUTHOR'S CORNER

Hello Everyone,

Before we begin, I just want to share a little about myself and why I am doing what I am doing.

I was born into a family of entrepreneurs in **Raipur, CG**, where business and innovation were part of my everyday upbringing.

My father, being **a first-generation entrepreneur and true inspirational leader in my life**, started his journey in the 1980s with not even **Rs. 50,000** (with no backing of business and no experience). Just through sheer grit, belief, and vision, he turned it into a **400+ crore empire**.

Growing up, I witnessed leaders transforming industries, proving that first-generation entrepreneurs could achieve extraordinary success through persistence and purpose. Inspired by such journeys, I knew I had to carve my own path, not just to expand my family's business but to create something meaningful that solves real-world problems, touches lives, and creates a bigger impact.

Ever since childhood, I've always found peace and harmony in nature. Forests, rivers, mountains, and valleys, these places don't just calm me; they uplift me. They remind me of abundance and balance. Too often, we don't realize the gift we've been given in the form of nature.

It makes me pause and reflect on how blessed we are to live in harmony with the environment and, at the same time, how much responsibility we have to protect it for our future generations. Over time, this love for nature evolved into a strong passion for contributing to sustainability, agriculture, smart irrigation, and providing efficient water management solutions.

The second important reason that keeps me in this zone is to improve and contribute, directly or indirectly, to the livelihood of the farming community.

As we know, farmers struggle to get access to resources because of various limitations, inefficient solutions, traditional methods, and remote locations that remain inaccessible.

And yet, **"they contribute more than 50% of India's population."**

This alone gives me immense power and responsibility to contribute to the farming community!

Empowering them isn't just an opportunity; it's our duty, as they thrive in India's growth journey too, that is what I believe! I never wanted to just run a business. I wanted to build a movement, one that creates real impact, uplifts communities, and grows with a win-win mindset.

This drives my mission to "Contribute to a Sustainable Future & Empower the Farmer Community."

After I completed my graduation from **Lancaster University, UK,**

I spent over a decade working across multiple business verticals:

Manufacturing, Polymers, Exports, and Irrigation & Water Management Solutions.

Each step taught me something new, but I still felt a calling for something more meaningful, which keeps me in MOJO!

The turning point came about **seven years ago**, in 2018, when I entered the **Solar Water Pumping Sector.**

It was a **Game Changer.**

For the first time, I saw how clean energy could **transform farmers' lives** while also making our planet greener and reducing carbon emissions.

Every installation we did **wasn't just a pump;**

it was a step towards sustainability, financial independence for farmers, and contributing to a better future for India.

The government's **PM-KUSUM scheme** became the most powerful initiative I had ever witnessed.

It wasn't just a scheme;

It was a movement. It provided farmers with an opportunity to use renewable energy, reduce diesel dependency, lower their input costs, and irrigate their lands more efficiently.

WHY THIS BOOK? WHY NOW?

Despite all the opportunities, I saw system integrators struggling. They had the vision but lacked the tools, the strategies, and the framework to scale up seamlessly.

Projects got delayed, profits shrank, and inefficiencies slowed what could've been extraordinary growth stories.

I've spent **7+ years serving India's leading organisations, EPCs, Solar Pumps & Panel Manufacturers, and Large System Integrators (SI)**, watching them succeed, struggle, and fail.

I've seen businesses grow 2X to 10X, but I've also seen promising companies shut down or exit the business because they didn't optimize their operations and other hidden aspects, along with various factors that stopped them from scaling.

This book is my way of helping or bringing awareness to system integrators to avoid costly mistakes and scale up their business seamlessly.

I just want to share my wide experience of 7+ years. I really want to help and contribute to the growth of SI system integrators, contribute to the success of the PM-KUSUM Yojana, and support India's growth journey in solar pumps.

That's why I created the **Unique Framework**, to help system integrators 2X their solar pump installations:

- Use the right materials to avoid costly failures
- Eliminate project delays and operational inefficiencies

- Grow without stress by mastering installation processes

This book is not just about solar pumps.

It is also about empowering entrepreneurs to contribute and create an impact in sustainability in the clean energy sector.

It's about helping system integrators grow hassle-free, increase profits, and contribute to a sustainable future.

In short, this book is your shortcut.

Your path to faster, making more money, doing it with confidence and peace of mind, and becoming a great contributor to opportunities in the PM-KUSUM Scheme.

Breaking a Few Misconceptions to Expand the Viewpoint Before We Begin (Not applicable for New Installers)

If you think you already know how to install pumps, you don't need a system.

Imagine two mechanics. Both know how to fix cars. But one has a systematic process, rightly organized with a step-by-step method, while the other?

He does things randomly, improvising as he goes, often taking twice the time.

Who do you think will make more money?

The same applies to solar pump installation.

Knowing the basics is different from mastering efficiency and profitability.

A system bridges that gap.

If you may think that government payments are slow; scaling will increase my risk!

Yes, it's true, subsidies and government payments can take time. But your business doesn't have to slow down.

The companies that manage cash flow smartly and optimize costs survive and thrive.

That's why scaling isn't just about more sales; it's about smarter systems.

If you think that bigger players dominate. I'm just a small integrator!

Some of the biggest names today started small.

The difference?

They didn't wait to become "big" before acting smart.

They optimized early, scaled with clarity, and positioned themselves strategically.

CHAPTER 1

The Revolution of Solar Pumping in India

> *"I'd put my money on the sun and solar energy. What a source of power! I hope we don't have to wait until oil and coal run out before we tackle that."* ***- Thomas Edison***

India is one of the world's **largest agricultural nations,** with over **50% of the population** depending on farming and allied activities.

However, there is one challenge that has persisted for decades, access to reliable and affordable irrigation.

Traditionally, **farmers have relied on diesel or electric pumps,** facing issues like:

- Unstable electricity supply in rural areas
- Rising fuel costs, making diesel pumps expensive
- **Limited water access due to inefficient irrigation methods**

To address these challenges, the government launched the **PM-KUSUM Scheme**, the world's **largest clean energy initiative for farmers,** designed to solarize **3.5 million agricultural pumps.**

Double Your Solar Pump Installations! Triple Your Profit

This initiative is transforming agriculture by making irrigation independent, affordable, and accessible and most importantly, giving control back to the farmer.

For all System Integrators, this presents a multi-billion-dollar opportunity. The combination of subsidies, increasing demand, and market expansion taking solar pumping industry for next level growth.

This is more than just a scheme; it's a silent revolution happening in India's farmlands, and integrators who align early will be writing the success stories of tomorrow.

Farmers are actively seeking solutions to break free from diesel dependency and high electricity costs. With increasing awareness and attractive subsidies under PM-KUSUM Yojana, the solar pumps are now in high demand.

Farmers getting **benefited up to 60%+** subsidy incentives depending on the state.

Standalone solar pumps, which work without electricity, are a perfect solution for remote areas.

Being a government-funded Scheme, this sector is protected from market volatility.

For SI (System Integrators) and KUSUM tender participants, this shift is a golden opportunity. The market is expanding rapidly, and those who position themselves early will dominate the sector. Those taking action are winning the game, not just tenders, they'll win trust, scale faster, and build long-term recurring revenue.

Don't Just Install - Create Long-Term Value

Most System Integrators make a critical mistake: they focus only on installations and ignore the long-term value chain.

- **Old Mindset:** "Just install the pump, take the margin, and move on."
- **The Smart Strategy:** "Maximize long-term revenue by installing quality standards components, service contracts & upselling opportunities."

The hidden profits in this business lie beyond the pump installation:

- **Quality Matters**: Components like corrosion-resistant, efficient controllers, and durable structures extend pump life and increase farmer satisfaction.
- **Post-Installation Services**: Installation done right, following the process and guidelines, minimizes post-installation issues. If not done correctly, costs rise and profits become invisible.
- **Brand & Reputation Growth**: Quality work on the ground leads to word-of-mouth marketing, opening doors to bigger tenders and collaborations. In rural markets, your reputation is your brand. Every satisfied farmer is your free marketing channel.

Think of solar pumps as a long-term business model, not a one-time sale.

They eat into your profits and hurt your long-term brand. Providing a guided installation will give the following outcomes:

- Better system performance
- Fewer service complaints

- Repeat business & referrals
- Higher lifetime value per customer

BoS is not a cost; it's an investment in reliability, trust, and future growth.

It's the difference between a one-time installer and a market leader.

CHAPTER 2

How Even 10% Can Become the Hidden Key to Accelerating Solar Pumping Installations?

> *"The bitterness of poor quality remains long after the sweetness of low price is forgotten."*
> ***- Benjamin Franklin***

ost system integrators and EPC companies have a vision to become leaders in their segment, but they get into a trap and loop from which it becomes difficult to come out. They act like operators, not managers, and get involved in coordinating a number of their vendors and associates for various items like solar panels, controllers, and pumps, believing these are the core of a solar pumping system.

While doing such coordination, they also get involved in small-value tasks, which kills their potential time and energy that could have been used for much higher output in company growth.

Imagine building a house with **the best walls, windows, and furniture but a weak foundation,** sooner or later, the structure will collapse.

The same applies to **solar pumping installations.**

- Strong coordination and selecting the right associates for procurement ensures seamless integration and installation of all components: solar panel, pump, controller, and cables working in perfect sync, enhancing installation speed, increasing farmer satisfaction, and significantly boosting your brand reputation.
- Poor associates and incorrect selection of components lead to inefficiencies, technical failures, and increased hidden maintenance costs that silently eat your profits.
- For system integrators and EPCs, mastering the difference between short-term profits and long-term dominance in the solar pumping business is crucial.

Why Must System Integrators Also Focus on BoS Kits?

Most EPCs **undervalue BoS kits** because they assume it's just a **small fraction of system costs (typically 10–15%).**

So, they outsource it to installers, but this increases risk and puts the work in doubt when it comes to a 5-year guarantee. Their PBG (Performance Bank Guarantee) is also with the government, and end-customer satisfaction is equally important to avoid complaints.

In reality, its impact on **performance, reliability, and scalability is huge.**

- **Customer Satisfaction**: A well-integrated system with quality BoS reduces farmer complaints and increases brand trust.
- **Service Calls & Replacements**: Cheap component selection breaks down quickly, leading to recurring site visits and invisible profit loss.

- **Maximized Project Efficiency –** Standardized and optimized components help in **faster installations, fewer technical issues, and better long-term performance.**

Example: Even a single miscellaneous faulty MC4 connector can delay an entire site by 2–3 days. Multiply that across 50 installations, and you've lost weeks of valuable revenue and momentum.

By investing in the right component selection and reliable associate partners, system integrators can increase installations, reduce maintenance costs, and gain a competitive edge.

Stop Thinking of BoS as Just "Extra Components"!

The Old Mindset: "BoS is just cables, pipes, and accessories. It doesn't need much attention."

The Smart Strategy: "BoS is the backbone of a solar pump installation.

Better quality = better efficiency, lower costs, and a long-lasting reputation."

To truly scale in solar pump installations, EPCs must:

- **Standardize BoS Selection**: Avoid low-quality components that cause frequent breakdowns.

  Build partnerships with reliable associates/vendors and create a benchmark of BoS standards and a quality checklist for your team to ensure consistency and durability across projects.

- **Focus on System Efficiency, Not Just Cost:**

  Cheap materials may save money upfront but cost more in long-term failures.

  Prioritize components that improve overall system performance and reduce maintenance efforts.

An illustration of how BoS balances the systems for seamless operation and integration.

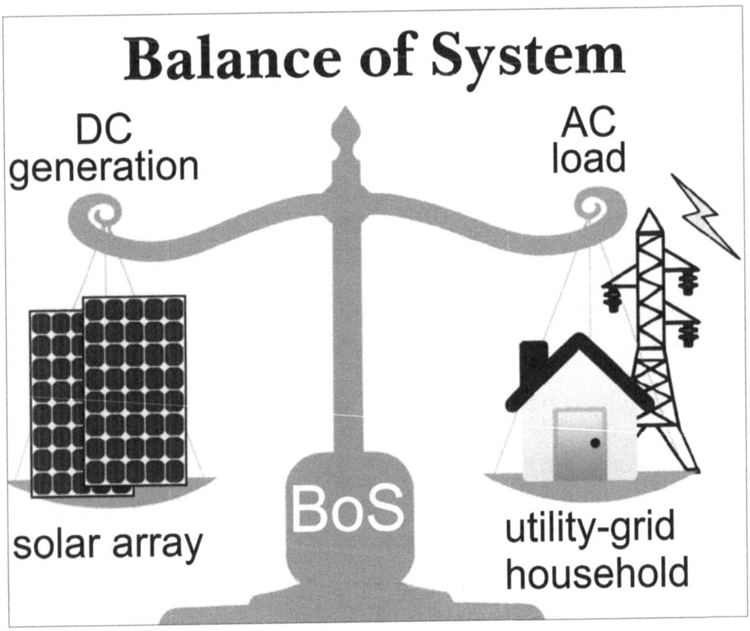

CHAPTER 3

The Unique Framework:
The Secret to Faster Growth in Solar Pumping

"It's not the will to win that matters, everyone has that. It's the will to prepare to win that matters."
– Paul "Bear" Bryant

Why I Created this Framework?

After working closely with system integrators and EPCs, I noticed that many of them faced the same challenges:

- ➢ Installations took longer than expected!
- ➢ Hidden costs were eating up profits!
- ➢ Repeated errors were causing delays and customer complaints!

Most of these problems had a common root, lack of structure and clarity.

Everyone was reinventing the wheel for every project. The absence of standard practices was leading to time waste, material loss, and miscommunication across teams.

I wanted to simplify the process and help system integrators save time, reduce costs, and grow effortlessly.

That's why I developed the **B.O.S. Framework,** a proven system to streamline solar pump installations and make businesses predictable, scalable, and more profitable.

Over time, this framework has been nothing short of a boon for many system integrators across India. Whether they were handling small installations or large-scale rural deployments, they reported fewer breakdowns, faster turnaround, and better client satisfaction; all thanks to this structured approach.

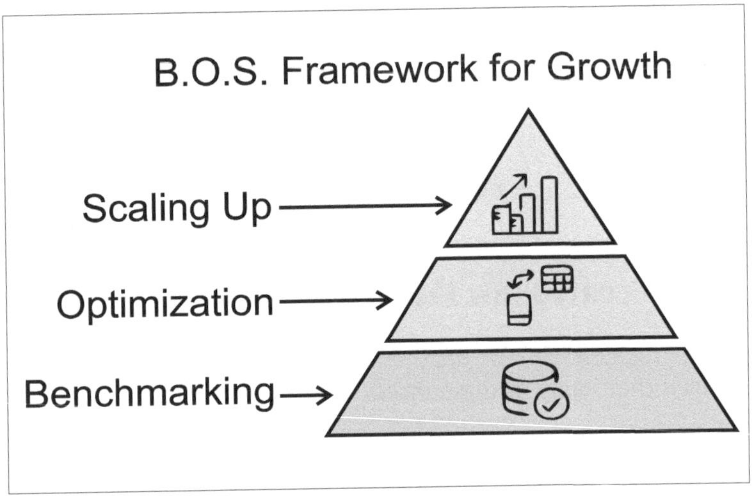

What is the B.O.S. Framework?

The B.O.S. Framework stands for:

B = Benchmarking → Setting quality standards for components and processes.

O = Optimization → Making the entire system cost-efficient, reducing hidden costs and delays.

S = Scaling Up → Using a structured approach to grow your business faster.

Formula for Success → B + O = S (Benchmarking + Optimization = Scalable Growth)

This isn't just theory. It's a hands-on, practical approach that helps you fix leaks in your system, be it in time, money, or manpower. From choosing the right small component to big components like standardizing controller installations and creating checklists for every site, the B.O.S. Framework puts control back in your hands.

It eliminates guesswork and assumptions, giving your entire team a blueprint for consistent execution.

What System Integrators Gain from the B.O.S. Framework

- **Faster Installations**: Well-optimized processes and high-quality components speed up installation, reducing project delays.
- **Lower Costs**: By cutting waste and avoiding unreliable materials, businesses save money in the long run.
- **Less Effort**: A well-planned system is easier to maintain and reduces the need for repairs or rework.

But that's not all. A structured approach also:

- **Boosts team productivity**: Technicians know exactly what to do, every time.
- **Reduces dependency on experts**: Because checklists and benchmarks guide even new team members.
- **Improves farmer satisfaction**: With timely, clean, and reliable installations that need minimal servicing.

By applying Benchmarking, Optimization, and Scaling, you're not just fixing pumps; you're building a professional, future-ready solar business.

This is the kind of clarity that turns a struggling integrator into a market leader.

CHAPTER 4

Let's Understand "B" - Benchmarking!

> *"Solar power is the last energy resource that isn't owned yet, nobody taxes the sun... yet."*
> ***– Bonnie Raitt***

As per Definition (Oxford/Google):

Benchmarking means evaluating something by comparison with a standard.

Definition: "Benchmarking means setting a standard and ensuring that all components and processes match or exceed that standard."

But why is benchmarking important for solar pumping?

Benchmarking isn't a luxury; it's a necessity for building a scalable and sustainable solar business. When you benchmark your components and processes, you:

- Prevent component failures
- Save money in the long run
- Improve installation speed build trust & brand reputation

1. Benchmarking in Components: Choosing the Right Parts

Selecting the right components is the foundation of a reliable solar pumping system. Your system is only as strong as its weakest part.

Why Poor Component Choices Lead to Problems:

- **Low-quality components underperform** and lead to loss and pump failure.
- **Mismatched controllers & pumps** reduce efficiency and cause breakdowns.

Key Areas for Benchmarking Components

- **Performance:** Every component should meet high standards in efficiency and durability.
- **Cost-Efficiency:** Cheaper isn't always better, investing in quality **saves money over time**.
- **Durability:** Choose components that can last at least **5 years+** without major issues.
- **Compatibility:** Ensure all parts **work seamlessly together** to avoid installation delays.
- **Reliable Suppliers:** Work only with **trusted suppliers** who provide **consistent quality** and **on-time delivery**.

Steps to Benchmark Components for Solar Pumps:

Step 1: Identify the Key Components

- Solar Panels
- Controllers
- Structures
- HDPE Pipes (BOS)
- Lightning Arrestors (LA) & Earthing (BOS)

- Cables & Wiring (BOS)
- Pumps (Submersible or Surface) (BOS)

Step 2: Define Each Component Standard Wise / Technical Spec Wise / Guideline Wise

- **Structures:** Must meet guideline specifications and galvanizing micros to ensure 5 years of lifespan and pass any surprise check.
- **Solar Panels:** Must meet energy efficiency norms and certification standards.
- **Pumps:** Discuss NRV sizes clearly with suppliers and buyers. Avoid last-minute surprises at the site due to mismatches.
- **HDPE Pipes:** Have specifications based on guidelines. Don't just copy; validate locally as per installer.
- **Cables & Wiring:** Must handle expected voltage loads without overheating. Insist on ISI-marked cables when possible.

Step 3: Compare Products & Suppliers

- **Research multiple suppliers** and compare quality, pricing, and service.
- **Check warranties** and **certifications** before making a final selection.
- Always do an *apple-to-apple comparison*, make sure you're comparing equal specifications.

Step 4: Select the Right Suppliers

- Prioritize quality, delivery speed, and after-sales support.
- Consider long-term partnerships for better pricing and reliable supply chains.

Step 5: Review Performance After Installation

- Track failures and repairs to identify weak links in the supply chain.
- Use this data to improve future component selection.

2. **Benchmarking in Processes & Training: Standardizing Installations**

Having a great product isn't enough, execution matters. Without proper installation processes and team training, even the best components can fail.

Why Standardized Processes Matter:

- **Prevents mistakes:** Clear guidelines mean fewer errors on-site.
- **Speeds up installations:** Teams know exactly what to do, reducing confusion and downtime.
- **Ensures consistency:** Every installation is done correctly, leading to **fewer service issues**.

How to Benchmark & Standardize the Installation Process

A successful solar pump business follows a predictable and repeatable process. Here's a sample standardized workflow that many top-performing integrators use:

Solar Pump Installation Workflow:

1. Order Received
2. Letter of Intent (LoI) Issued
3. Site Survey Conducted
4. Material Requisition & Procurement
5. Installation Begins
6. Government Inspection (JCR Filing)
7. Payment Processed

Why This Works: Following this structured approach reduces delays minimizes rework, and creates a professional image. Most importantly, it results in faster installations and quicker payments, keeping both clients and teams happy.

Training: Turning Installers into Experts

Your process is only as good as the people executing it. That's where training comes in. Without proper training, even a well-documented process will fail.

Why Training Matters:

- New installers learn faster, reducing dependency on experienced workers.
- Common mistakes are avoided, saving both time and money.
- Quality of work improves, leading to fewer service calls and greater customer satisfaction.

Well-trained teams reflect professionalism and build a stronger brand.

TIPS

Leading companies like Tata Power Solar, Rotomag Motors and Controllers, and many others have invested heavily in detailed training manuals, demo sessions, and SOPs.

Their teams are trained to follow step-by-step guides that ensure even fresh installers can handle tasks with confidence.

Importantly, these guides help avoid small mistakes, like improper cable fittings or pump alignment, that can lead to big problems and hidden costs later.

CHAPTER 5

"O" Optimization - Making the System Efficient

> *"Efficiency is doing things right; effectiveness is doing the right things."*
> ***- Peter Drucker***

Optimization means improving how you use Time, Resources, and Inventory to increase profits.

How Optimization Helps:

- **Saves Time:** Reduces waiting time for materials and installations.
- **Reduces Costs**: Eliminates wastage in materials and operations.
- **Faster Project Completion**: Complete more projects in less time = More profits and quicker payments.

5.1 Optimization in Time: Focus on What Matters Most

Apply the Pareto Principle (80/20 Rule): 80% of business growth comes from **20% of key activities**. Focus on **high-impact /value work.**

Example: Many system integrators **waste 40–50% of their time** coordinating with multiple suppliers for multiple small-value components. This takes their potential time and energy, which does not help their profits, but they could have achieved much better profits by increasing installations effortlessly.

Reducing Installation Delays

- **Plan installations a few days in advance** – Avoid last-minute site issues, but do ensure the right quantity as per the requirement with specific pump outlets and other components.
- **Ensure components arrive on-site together** – Reduces missing parts and waiting time.
- **Follow a strict TAT (Turnaround Time) for installations** – Ensures quicker completion and payment processing.

5.2 Optimization in Resources: Managing Supply Chains & Logistics

How System Integrators Can Optimize Resources:

1. **Single vs. Multi-Source Procurement**

   Single-Source Procurement:

   - **Faster deliveries**: It ensures everything arrives at once, simplified logistics and faster deliveries, reducing lead times.
   - **Better compatibility**: It also takes accountability to ensure compatibility among components, reducing the risk of mismatches and installation errors, Easier to manage warranties and service agreements from one source.
   - **Simplifies logistics**: Reduces coordination issues.

Multi-Source Procurement:

- **More price flexibility**: Can get cheaper deals on specific items.
- **Increases complexity**: Harder to coordinate deliveries, difficulties in coordinating multiple deliveries.
- **Higher risk of compatibility issues**: Different brands may not integrate well, higher risk of component incompatibility.

Best Strategy: Use Single-Source Procurement for faster installations and smoother operations.

2. **Maintain a Buffer Stock for Critical Components**

   Why? Avoids unexpected delays if suppliers face shortages. **Key Items to Keep in Stock:** Pipes, cables, connectors, fasteners, and controllers.

   A buffer today can prevent a backlog tomorrow.

5.3 Optimization in Inventory Management

Hidden Profits in Inventory Management:

Many companies lose money due to poor inventory control, leading to stock shortages, delays, and theft from their remote areas.

Best Practices:

- **Just-In-Time (JIT) Inventory System**: Order materials only as per site requirement. Helps reduce unnecessary locking of funds.
- **Regular Inventory Audits**: Track stock levels weekly to prevent missing parts.

- **Warehouse Security & Accountability**: Assign team leads to manage local store records. Keep access limited. Use locks & cameras, if possible, in remote yards.

How This Helps: Reduces capital tied up in excess inventory, improves cash flow, and keeps projects moving smoothly.

Final Thoughts: Why Benchmarking & Optimization Lead to Success

System integrators who benchmark components, optimize processes, and manage inventory smartly can:

- **Install solar pumps at least 3x faster time,** as demonstrated by the top players in the solar pump industry. Their performance records prove that efficiency in benchmarking and optimization leads to significantly quicker installations.
- **Reduce costly mistakes and maintenance issues,** ensuring smoother operations and higher customer satisfaction.
- **Increase profits without increasing workload,** streamlining operations and minimizing waste, so you can grow without burnout.

Tips

The top 10 companies lead 60–70% of solar pump executions under the KUSUM scheme. These industry leaders primarily rely on sourcing major items such as structures, panels, pumps, controllers, and BoS from trusted suppliers.

They've mastered the art of outsourcing components with reliability, using their own strict evaluation criteria. This allows them to focus on what matters most: driving business growth, enhancing customer experience, and streamlining operations.

CHAPTER 6

Scaling Up - The Smart Way to Grow Your Solar Pump Business

"Growth is painful. Change is painful. But nothing is as painful as staying stuck somewhere you don't belong."

- N.R. Narayana Murthy

Scaling up doesn't just mean increasing installations; it means growing profitably and sustainably. Many system integrators rush to expand, only to face operational bottlenecks, cash flow problems, and declining service quality that hurt their brand.

True scaling happens when three key elements are in place:

➢ **Operational Efficiency**: Faster, smoother installations with fewer delays.

- **Customer Satisfaction**: More referrals, repeat business, and a strong brand.
- **Profitability**: Higher margins, smarter resource use, and consistent cash flow.

Scaling is the reward for mastering Benchmarking & Optimization. If these foundations aren't strong, expansion can lead to chaos instead of success.

The Right Way to Scale Up by Avoiding the Common Mistakes

Many system integrators make the mistake of expanding too quickly without having the right systems in place, right control. This leads to:

- **Delayed Projects**: More projects, but not enough skilled teams to deliver.
- **Poor Quality Installations**: Rushed work leads to farmer complaints, service calls, & damage to your reputation.
- **Financial Strain**: Growing too fast without managing cash flow leads to payment delays, credit issues, and stalled operations.

Smart Solution: Scale with Strategy!

Successful system integrators don't just chase volume.

They focus on **making every project smoother, faster, and more profitable** and *then* scale from a position of strength.

Before Scaling, Ask Yourself:

1. Are my installations consistently efficient and error-free?
2. Is my team trained and ready to handle more projects without compromising quality?

3. Do I have a solid inventory and procurement system that won't break under pressure?
4. Is my cash flow stable enough to support growth?

Ever Thought About How to Scale Effortlessly?

Scaling your solar pump business isn't about *doing more,* it's about *doing better,* and making growth automatic. Here's how top-performing System Integrators (SIs) scale smartly **without burning out or overspending**.

1. **By Building a Trust & Credibility**

   Want to know how leading companies get **3X more projects** without extra marketing?

   They don't run after farmers... **farmers come to them. How?**

   - **Faster installations + problem-free service** → Farmers spread the word.
   - **Government appreciation** → Leads to more visibility & higher chances of winning new projects.
   - **Long-term reliability** → Gets them repeat orders from agencies & higher budgets.

   Example: Companies leading in solar pumping & large solar power projects follow Benchmarking & Optimization to ensure smooth operations. This naturally leads to effortless farmer selections & brand recognition.

   When your reputation speaks louder than your ads, *scaling becomes automatic.*

2. **Fast & Quality Installations: The Winning Combo**

   The biggest mistake? Scaling up without fixing inefficiencies first.

- **Problem:** Many system integrators take on too many projects, leading to delays, errors, and financial loss.
- **Solution:** Build a process where every installation follows a structured workflow.

What Top System Integrators Do Differently:

- **Standardized installation methods**: No confusion, no wasted time.
- Work with **pre-approved suppliers & BoS components**: No last-minute procurement delays.
- **Trained installation teams**: Less supervision, faster work.

Scaling isn't about doing more work; it's about doing work faster & smarter.

3. **Optimize Your Cash Flow to Handle More Projects**
    - **Common Issue:** System integrators struggle with cash flow when government payments are delayed.
    - **Smart Strategy:** Secure projects with strong payment cycles & supplier credit terms.

    How to Improve Cash Flow While Scaling:

    - **Diversify revenue streams**: Offer post-installation maintenance services.
    - **Plan payments carefully**: Ensure projects don't stop due to cash shortages.

Scaling up is easier when financial risks are minimized.

The Growth Mindset

> **Old Mindset:** "If I take on more projects, I'll make more money."

- **New Mindset:** "If I make installations smoother & faster, growth will happen naturally."

How to Think Like a Market Leader

- **Stop micromanaging every project →** Build a trusted team that follows a systematic approach.
- **Think beyond a one-time sale →** Offer long-term service contracts that generate recurring income and customer loyalty.
- **Focus on building relationships, not just closing sales →** Farmers & agencies should see you as a trusted expert, not just a supplier or contractor.

Scaling happens when you build a business that runs efficiently, even without you handling every detail.

Common Myths That Stop System Integrators from Scaling Up

1. **I Don't Have Enough Manpower to Scale Up?**

   Reality Check: Many leading EPC companies don't have large teams; they just have well-trained teams.

   Solution: Instead of hiring more people, train existing workers to follow a step-by-step installation guide for consistency and speed.

   Insight: It's about quality, not quantity. Focusing on skill development and efficient workflows can boost your team's productivity without increasing headcount.

2. **Government Payments Are Too Slow, How to Expand?**

   Reality Check: The top 10 fastest-growing solar pump companies still rely on government projects but they **manage their cash flow wisely.**

Solution

- Work with suppliers who offer flexible payment terms.
- Take on smaller projects with faster payments while waiting for larger payments.

Insight: Balancing short-term projects with larger ones ensures consistent cash flow, even when facing delayed government payments. Smart financial management is the key to scaling.

3. **I Already Have Enough Work, Do I still Need to Scale?**

   Reality Check: Businesses that don't scale become stagnant and eventually lose market share.

   Solution: Scaling isn't about just getting bigger; it's about getting better. Even if you don't want to double your installations, you can scale profits by optimizing efficiency and reducing costs.

   Insight: Scaling is about improving your operations. It doesn't always mean expanding your workforce, sometimes, it's about maximizing the potential of what you already have.

The Fastest-Growing System Integrators Follow These Steps

- **They focus on brand reputation first**, they don't chase customers, customers come to them.
- **They have structured installation systems** which makes installation fast, smooth, and problem-free execution.
- **They manage cash flow smàrtly**, so that projects keep moving, even if payments are delayed.
- **They focus on first-time success** – no costly rework or site revisits.

- **They build long-term relationships** with government agencies, suppliers and also making their end customer (farmer) satisfied with their service.
- **They reduce project delays**, as time is money, and faster installations mean more earnings.

Final Thoughts: Scaling Up is About More Than Just Growth

Many companies have doubled or tripled their revenues and profits just by following this approach.

The choice is yours:

- Keep working hard without major growth, constantly fixing problems as they appear, **OR**
- Build a system that grows your business effortlessly, freeing your time while multiplying your results.

Remember, scaling is a mindset; it's about thinking strategically, optimizing what you have, and creating a business that runs efficiently and profitably.

Even small changes, like using checklists, standardizing components, or training your team better can lead to massive results over time.

Build something that works while you sleep, sells while you plan, and grows while you lead.

CHAPTER 7

Minimizing Hidden Costs & Unlocking Hidden Profits

> *"Don't focus on the profits. Focus on the value you provide. Profit is just the by-product."*
> ***– Marty Neumeier***

1. **Think Beyond Just "Low-Cost" Materials**

   Old Thinking: "If I buy cheaper components, I will save money."

   New Thinking: "If I buy the right components, I will save money in the long run."

   Many integrators believe **buying the cheapest components** is a smart move. But in reality:

   - Underperforming components lead to replacements and extra labour costs, causing system failures and repairs.
   - Hidden costs often show up after 3–6 months. By then, the savings from cheaper components are already wiped out by repair costs and reputational damage.

   The Smart Strategy? Invest in Quality from the Start!

   - **Standard Components = Fewer repairs & replacements** → Lower long-term costs.

- **Reliable Suppliers = Faster deliveries & no compatibility issues** → No project delays.
- **Standardized Components = Easier installations** → Less labor & faster project completion.

Smart system integrators invest in efficiency, not just low prices.

2. **Speeding Up Installations**

Every extra day on-site adds unnecessary costs and can create scheduling chaos if you're managing multiple projects.

How to Speed Up Installations:

- **Pre-installation planning**: Ensure materials & manpower are ready before starting work.
- **Work with one-stop suppliers**: Avoid delays caused by multiple vendor deliveries.
- **Use standardized components**: Easier & faster installation with fewer errors.
- **Train installers properly**: Reduces mistakes, rework, and project delays.

Time is money. Reducing installation time by even one day per site can free up resources for your next project, giving you a competitive edge without increasing overhead.

Faster installations = More completed projects = More profits!

3. **Reduce Rework & Site Revisits (Do it Right the First Time!)**

Revisiting a site due to **installation errors or component failures** is a **huge hidden cost**.

How to Avoid Rework Costs:

- **Train your installation teams**: Less chance of errors, reducing rework.
- **Use high-quality components**: Fewer failures, fewer site revisits.
- **Follow standard installation guidelines**: Prevents short-term and long-term system issues.

Every site revisit is not just a cost; it's a branding loss. The farmer no longer recommends you. One small mistake can erase the trust built through marketing and word-of-mouth.

Fewer revisits mean lower transport & labor costs, leading to higher profits!

Final Thoughts: Hidden Profits Are Already in Your Business

- Every day of delay costs money.
- Every poor-quality component leads to future expenses.
- Every rework or site revisit reduces your profits.

Imagine this: If you could reduce just one site revisit per month, cut installation time by 1 day, and avoid even two component failures, you'd **save thousands per year**, with zero extra marketing or manpower.

This is the **power of attention to detail**, and the beauty of process thinking.

The hidden profits have always been there. You just needed the lens to see them.

The system integrators who control hidden costs don't just work hard, they work smart. And the most profitable ones? They treat efficiency as a growth strategy.

Message From the Author

When I first created the B.O.S. framework, I never imagined how deeply it would impact the Indian solar pump business. Over the years, I've had the privilege of sharing this tool with hundreds of system integrators, and seeing their success stories unfold has been nothing short of incredible.

Many of them have gone on to generate multi-crore profits, and I can proudly say that the B.O.S. framework has truly been a game-changer for the industry. For me, it's more than just a business strategy; it's my tool, my magic, and it's helping me accomplish my mission to make the solar industry more efficient, profitable, and sustainable.

It fills me with immense joy and pride when I hear about businesses thriving, teams growing, and our country progressing because of the impact of this framework. Every day, I get to learn that somewhere, someone is building a better business, leading a stronger team, and contributing to a brighter future. This is what keeps me motivated and gives me a deep sense of happiness.

As I continue on this journey, I hope the B.O.S. framework serves as a stepping stone for more entrepreneurs to take their businesses to the next level, just as it has for many before. Together, we are growing not just businesses, but revolutionizing the solar ecosystem in India.

Well, Coming to an End...

I have shared my experience, and many system integrators are growing with this approach.

To take more value out and discover how you can scale your solar pump installations faster and smarter, I would love to invite you for a one-on-one Zoom session.

You can write to me at: anirudh@oceanplus.co.in

This short meeting could open up simple strategies that may help you achieve 3x faster results, also hassle-free.

Let's connect and discover how we can help scale your business with ease and joy.